ABUNDANT TRUTH INTERNATIONAL MINISTRIES

Prophetic Studies Series

PROPHETIC FOUNDATIONS

An Introduction to the Gift of Prophecy

Roderick Levi Evans

Published by Abundant Truth Publishing
P.O. Box 126
Camden, NC 27921
Web: www.abundantpublishing.net
Email: abundantpublishing@gmail.com

Printed U.S.A.

Front & Back Cover Designs by Abundant Truth Publishing
All rights reserved.
Image by Bernd from Pixabay

Abundant Truth Publishing is a ministry of **Abundant Truth International Ministries.** The primary mission of ATI Ministries is to equip the Body of Christ with tools necessary to defend and contend for the truth of the Christian faith. Jesus Christ came to bear witness of the truth and ATI Ministries is a modern-day extension of His commission (John 18:37).

Prophetic Foundations: An Introduction to the Gift of Prophecy
©2025 Abundant Truth Publishing
All Rights Reserved
ISBN: 978-1-60141-669-8

Unless otherwise indicated, all of the scripture quotations are taken from the *Authorized King James Version* of the Bible. Scripture quotations marked with NIV are taken from the *New International Version* of the Bible. Scripture quotations marked with NASV are taken from the *New American Standard Version* of the Bible. Scripture quotations marked with Amplified are taken from the *Amplified Bi*

Printed in the United States of America

Contents

Preface

Introduction

Chapter 1 – The Prophetic Determination   1

Distinguishing Prophecy   3
Defining Prophecy   4

Chapter 2 – The Gift of Prophecy   9

Realizing Prophecy   11
Reasons for Prophecy   12

Chapter 3 – The Prophetic Office and Anointing   17

Understanding the Difference   19
Understanding the Demonstration   20

Contents (cont.)

Understanding the Prophetic Office   21

Chapter 4 – The Spirit of Prophecy   27

The Testimony of Jesus   29
The Testimony of the Assembly   30
The Testimony's Progression   32

Bibliography   37

Scriptural Appendix   39

The Outpouring of the Spirit   43
(Acts 2:17-18)
The Nine Gifts of the Spirit   45
(I Corinthians 12:4-11)
The Setting of Gifts in the Church   47
(I Corinthians 12:27-28)

Contents (cont.)

The Gift of Togues versus Prophecy	*49*
(I Corinthians 14:1-9)	
Protocol for Tongues and Prophecy	*53*
(I Corinthians 14:27-33)	
Other Ministries/Gifts of the Spirit	*55*
(Romans 12:4-8)	
The Ministry Gifts and Purpose	*57*
(Ephesians 4:11-15)	

Preface

The gift of prophecy is an important gift in the Church. God uses this gift to reveal His mind and heart to His people. However, there are individuals because of immaturity, pride, and other various reasons that have mishandled the use of this gift. This has caused misery in the lives of some believers.

I wrote this book to clarify the purpose of the gift of prophecy and prophetic ministry. It provides foundational information for further study of this gift.

This work comes from a desire to see the Body of Christ grounded in the function of the prophetic gift. I, personally, have been blessed by this gift and want to see others trust in its operation.

Roderick Levi Evans

Introduction

The promise of the Father was the outpouring of the Holy Spirit. In Joel's prophecy, he said the prophetic revelation, dreams, and visions would be the outward demonstration of Spirit's coming. Therefore, prophetic revelation and ministry is a permanent feature of the New Testament Church.

The Prophetic Studies Series was designed to inform and encourage the believer in prophetic manifestations and demonstrations in the Church. It is our prayer that believers will acknowledge, accept, and appreciate the prophetic ministry today.

In this publication:

Controversy over the gifts and ministries of the Spirit has abounded for centuries. Various scholars have taught that there was a cessation of the gifts. More specifically, they affirm that the gifts of the Spirit as listed in I Corinthians 12 are no longer in operation nor valid.

However, in recent years, a resurgence of the operation and demonstration of the gifts has occurred. Traditional and Non-traditional churches, alike, have experienced the visitation of God through the Holy Spirit.

Since the emergence and acceptance of the gifts of the Holy Spirit, various authors have written concerning this phenomenon. In spite of this, many in the Church, presently, do not understand the functions and operations of the gifts.

One gift among these that cause great controversy is the gift of prophecy. Even in organizations and denominations that consider the gifts valid today, comprehension is oftentimes elementary.

Where there is no clear understanding, individuals become vulnerable to deception and error. Since the gift of prophecy is an awesome gift, there are individuals in the Church who desire to have this gift.

There are men and women who know they do not have this gift, yet they pursue it. They lust after the respect that men have for those who possess this gift. This has produced erroneous prophetic ministry in the Church. Many lives have been negatively influenced. Misery was a product of these mishaps in ministry.

The focus of this book is to serve as an introduction to the gift of prophecy, prophetic operations, and to the pitfalls associated with prophetic ministry. This information will help individuals to rediscover the purpose of the prophetic gift in the Church. It is our hope that believers will develop a greater respect and appreciation for the inspiration, revelation, and power of the Holy Spirit in the Body of Christ.

THE GIFT OF PROPHECY An Introduction to the Prophetic Gift

-Chapter 1-
The Prophetic Determination

THE GIFT OF PROPHECY
An Introduction to the Prophetic Gift

THE GIFT OF PROPHECY   An Introduction to the Prophetic Gift

Thus saith the Lord." This is an expression that some believers cannot wait to hear and an expression that some despise. In spite of these feelings, God has placed this gift in the body of Christ. It is not only reserved for those who are prophets, but for any believer whom the Spirit will use.

Distinguishing Prophecy

It is a widely publicized gift, but many are still confused about its use, function, and purpose.

The Greek word for 'to prophesy' is 'propheteuo.' It means to foretell events and speak under divine inspiration. This means that the source of prophecy is God.

No one can prophesy except the Lord gives the revelation. Prophetic ministry is interwoven throughout the Old Testament. There are different Hebrew words used to describe prophecy.

Defining Prophecy

Two prevalent words are 'Raba' and 'Nataf.' Each describes a different aspect of prophecy. Raba means to pour forth or spurt. This speaks of the oftentimes spontaneous method in which prophecy is received and administered.

THE GIFT OF PROPHECY An Introduction to the Prophetic Gift

Numerous accounts tell of the prophetic spirit coming suddenly on individuals to deliver God's message. Nataf means to drop or rain heavily. This speaks of the source of the prophecy. This demonstrates that the prophetic word comes from God above, like the rain does from the sky.

THE GIFT OF PROPHECY
An Introduction to the Prophetic Gift

THE GIFT OF PROPHECY
An Introduction to the Prophetic Gift

Notes:

THE GIFT OF PROPHECY
An Introduction to the Prophetic Gift

-Chapter 2-

The Gift of Prophecy

THE GIFT OF PROPHECY An Introduction to the Prophetic Gift

THE GIFT OF PROPHECY An Introduction to the Prophetic Gift

In its simplest form to prophesy means to speak for God under divine inspiration.

Realizing Prophecy

When someone gives a word of prophecy, it must be a "now" word; meaning, the word should be coming fresh from God. Some things that we call prophecy are really the word of knowledge or the word of wisdom in operation.

Prophecy can be predictive, but this is not its main function. Prophecy is designed to help the believer know what is the mind and heart of God. Prophecy serves as a testimony of the Lord Jesus Christ being in the midst of His people (Revelation 19:10).

Paul instructed the believers to covet the best gifts, especially prophecy. Prophecy is a direct word from the Lord. It does not come from intuition, feelings, or thought. It comes from the Spirit of the Lord.

Reasons for Prophecy

Whether through a prophet or layman, prophecy always comes with a purpose. In the most basic terms, prophecy comes with edification, exhortation, and comfort.

But one who prophesies speaks to men for edification, exhortation, and consolation. One who speaks in a tongue edifies himself; but one who prophesies edifies the church. (I Corinthians 14:3-4 NASV)

Edify means to erect, build, or construct. When a word of prophecy is spoken, it should help to build up or strengthen believers in their walk with the Lord.

Exhort means to encourage or provoke an action. Many associate exhortation with encouragement only. Though this is true, but there is another side to exhortation. Sometimes, exhortation is given that the people of God may repent and change their ways. The prophetic message may contain elements of rebuke through exhortation.

Comfort means to succor, help, or soothe. Oftentimes, the word of prophecy comes with a demonstration of the love and care of God for His people. This causes believers to be comforted in their trials, tests, and struggles. Whenever a word of prophecy is given, it should accomplish at least one of these three.

THE GIFT OF PROPHECY An Introduction to the Prophetic Gift

Notes:

-Chapter 3-

The Prophetic Office and Anointing

THE GIFT OF PROPHECY An Introduction to the Prophetic Gift

There are individuals in the Church who are not prophets, but there is a definite prophetic touch on their lives and ministries. These individuals are said to possess a prophetic anointing. How does this differ from someone who has the gift of prophecy?

Understanding the Difference

In simple terms, the person who has the gift of prophecy will prophesy on occasion. However, an individual with a prophetic anointing will prophesy frequently as they minister to the Body of Christ.

Possessing a prophetic anointing does not place one in the office of the prophet, but it does make them one of the sons (or daughters) of the prophets.

In the scriptures, the sons of the prophets would prophesy, but not with the same level of influence as those called to the prophetic office such as Jeremiah, Elijah, Ezekiel, Joel, and others.

Understanding the Demonstration

The prophetic anointing is seen oftentimes in believers who are called to the five-fold ministry. They will operate in their respective offices while exercising prophetic insight and authority. The prophetic anointing adds a depth and dimension to their ministries.

In addition, one does not have to be called to a ministry office to possess a prophetic anointing. These individuals are strategically placed in the Body of Christ that all may be partakers of the prophetic ministry. Individuals who possess a prophetic anointing will prophesy frequently.

They will have dreams and visions consistently. In addition, they will be able to recognize and discern the word of the Lord for a particular situation.

Understanding the Prophetic Office

Every believer is a candidate for the gift

of prophecy. However, what makes the ministry of the prophet different from other believers who prophesy? The answer to this question is simple.

The prophecy of the prophet will provide direction, give insight into purpose, rebuke, correct, and reveal future events in God's eternal purpose.

This is in addition to edification, exhortation, and comfort. When the prophet ministers, the prophecies will be of greater depth, dimension, and clarity.

The prophet's ministry is foundational. The prophecies of the prophet will often include revelation concerning the will of God for an individual's life and ministry.

Also, the prophetic ministry of the prophet will reveal areas of spiritual weakness; including areas of spiritual warfare. The prophet's revelation will be of a greater strength even of those who possess a prophetic anointing.

THE GIFT OF PROPHECY
An Introduction to the Prophetic Gift

THE GIFT OF PROPHECY — An Introduction to the Prophetic Gift

Notes:

THE GIFT OF PROPHECY
An Introduction to the Prophetic Gift

-Chapter 4-

The Spirit of Prophecy

THE GIFT OF PROPHECY An Introduction to the Prophetic Gift

The greatest expression of prophecy is not in the gift of prophecy or in the prophetic anointing. It is in the spirit of prophecy.

The Testimony of Jesus

The scriptures reveal that the spirit of prophecy is the testimony of Jesus.

And I fell at his feet to worship him. And he said unto me, See thou do it not: I am thy fellowservant, and of thy brethren that have the testimony of Jesus: worship God: for the testimony of Jesus is the spirit of prophecy. (Revelation 19:10)

In the Book of Revelation, the testimony of Jesus was the affirmation of Christ's death, burial, resurrection, and supremacy. The spirit of prophecy represents the Church's proclamation to the world of Christ. How does this affect the local assembly?

The Testimony of the Assembly

When the spirit of prophecy is manifested in an assembly, any believer present will be able to prophesy even if he/she does not have the gift of prophecy or a prophetic anointing. The spirit of prophecy comes to unify the Church so that the Church represents one voice to any unbelievers that

THE GIFT OF PROPHECY — An Introduction to the Prophetic Gift

are present. Paul alludes to the spirit of prophecy in his letter to the Corinthians.

But if all prophesy, and there come in one that believeth not, or one unlearned, he is convinced of all, he is judged of all. (I Corinthians 14:24)

The only time all believers will be able to prophesy at once is when the spirit of prophecy is present. Paul writes that the unbeliever is judged of all.

This means that the unbeliever is faced with the reality of God. This is how the spirit of prophecy is Jesus' testimony. The unbeliever will not be able to deny God's existence through its manifestation.

> *And thus are the secrets of his heart made manifest; and so falling down on his face he will worship God, and report that God is in you of a truth. (I Corinthians 14:25*

The Testimony's Progression

The prophetic progression from the gift of prophecy to the spirit of prophecy is comparable to an ocean's geography. The further one goes out, the deeper the water becomes. Prophecy manifests in a similar manner. The prophetic gift is in the shallow

THE GIFT OF PROPHECY An Introduction to the Prophetic Gift

part of the ocean. Then it gets deeper as one operates in the prophetic anointing and office.

This comparison provides the basis for a general warning regarding the prophetic. One must remember to operate in the measure of the prophetic that God gives them.

In the analogy, the further one goes out in the ocean, the deeper the water becomes. If one operates beyond their measure, they will drown; that is, go into error and kill the prophetic that is within them. Remember, do not try to operate in a prophetic realm for which God has not called you.

Now that we have addressed what is prophecy, a clear view of what is not prophecy is obtainable. In the next chapter, we will examine the ways in which prophecy is delivered; that is, the prophetic vehicle.

THE GIFT OF PROPHECY An Introduction to the Prophetic Gift

Notes:

THE GIFT OF PROPHECY
An Introduction to the Prophetic Gift

Bibliography

Evans, Roderick Levi. (2012). The Prophetic Mantle: The Gift of Prophecy and Prophetic Operations in the Church Today Abundant Truth Publishing. Camden, NC, 2014

Lockman Foundation. *Comparative Study Bible.* Zondervan Publishing House. Grand Rapids, MI, c1984

Merriam-Webster Online Dictionary

Copyright © 2005 by Merriam-Webster, Incorporated. All rights reserved.

The Bible Library. *The Bible Library CD Rom Disc.* Ellis Enterprises Incorporated, (c) 1988 – 2000. 4205 McAuley Blvd., Suite 385, Oklahoma City, OK 73120. All Rights Reserved.

Scriptural Appendix

THE GIFT OF PROPHECY An Introduction to the Prophetic Gift

THE GIFT OF PROPHECY An Introduction to the Prophetic Gift

The ministry of the prophet and the prophetic gift of the Spirit are a source of controversy and excitement. This appendix lists some popular passages of scriptures concerning ministries and gifts. These are given to inspire others to research this topic.

THE GIFT OF PROPHECY An Introduction to the Prophetic Gift

The Outpouring of the Spirit
(Acts 2:17-18)

17. And it shall come to pass in the last days, saith God, I will pour out of my Spirit upon all flesh: and your sons and your daughters shall prophesy, and your young men shall see visions, and your old men shall dream dreams:

18. And on my servants and on my handmaidens I will pour out in those days of my Spirit; and they shall prophesy:

THE GIFT OF PROPHECY An Introduction to the Prophetic Gift

THE GIFT OF PROPHECY An Introduction to the Prophetic Gift

The Nine Gifts of the Spirit
(I Corinthians 12:4-11)

4. Now there are diversities of gifts, but the same Spirit.

5. And there are differences of administrations, but the same Lord.

6. And there are diversities of operations, but it is the same God which worketh all in all.

7. But the manifestation of the Spirit is given to every man to profit withal.

8. For to one is given by the Spirit the word of wisdom; to another the word of knowledge by the same Spirit;

9. To another faith by the same Spirit; to another the gifts of healing by the same Spirit;

10. To another the working of miracles; to another prophecy; to another discerning of spirits; to another divers kinds of tongues; to another the interpretation of tongues:

11. But all these worketh that one and the selfsame Spirit, dividing to every man severally as he will.

The Setting of Gifts in the Church (I Corinthians 12:27-28)

27. Now ye are the body of Christ, and members in particular.

28. And God hath set some in the church, first apostles, secondarily prophets, thirdly teachers, after that miracles, then gifts of healings, helps, governments, diversities of tongues.

THE GIFT OF PROPHECY
An Introduction to the Prophetic Gift

THE GIFT OF PROPHECY An Introduction to the Prophetic Gift

The Gift of Togues versus Prophecy
(I Corinthians 14:1-9)

1. Follow after charity, and desire spiritual gifts, but rather that ye may prophesy.

2. For he that speaketh in an unknown tongue speaketh not unto men, but unto God: for no man understandeth him; howbeit in the spirit he speaketh mysteries.

3. But he that prophesieth speaketh unto men to edification, and exhortation, and comfort.

4. He that speaketh in an unknown tongue edifieth himself; but he that prophesieth

edifieth the church.

5. I would that ye all spake with tongues; but rather that ye prophesied: for greater is he that prophesieth than he that speaketh with tongues, except he interpret, that the church may receive edifying.

6. Now, brethren, if I come unto you speaking with tongues, what shall I profit you, except I shall speak to you either by revelation, or by knowledge, or by prophesying, or by doctrine?

7. And even things without life giving sound, whether pipe or harp, except they give a distinction in the sounds, how shall it be

known what is piped or harped?

8. For if the trumpet give an uncertain sound, who shall prepare himself to the battle?

9. So likewise ye, except ye utter by the tongue words easy to be understood, how shall it be known what is spoken? for ye shall speak into the air.

THE GIFT OF PROPHECY An Introduction to the Prophetic Gift

Protocol for Tongues and Prophecy

(I Corinthians 14:27-33)

27. If any man speak in an unknown tongue, let it be by two, or at the most by three, and that by course; and let one interpret.

28. But if there be no interpreter, let him keep silence in the church; and let him speak to himself, and to God.

29. Let the prophets speak two or three, and let the other judge.

30. If any thing be revealed to another that

sitteth by, let the first hold his peace.

31. For ye may all prophesy one by one, that all may learn, and all may be comforted.

32. And the spirits of the prophets are subject to the prophets.

33. For God is not the author of confusion, but of peace, as in all churches of the saints.

Other Ministries/Gifts of the Spirit (Romans 12:4-8)

4. For as we have many members in one body, and all members have not the same office:

5. So we, being many, are one body in Christ, and every one members one of another.

6. Having then gifts differing according to the grace that is given to us, whether prophecy, let us prophesy according to the proportion of faith;

7. Or ministry, let us wait on our ministering: or he that teacheth, on teaching;

8. Or he that exhorteth, on exhortation: he that giveth, let him do it with simplicity; he that ruleth, with diligence; he that sheweth mercy, with cheerfulness.

The Ministry Gifts and Purpose

(Ephesians 4:11-15)

11. And he gave some, apostles; and some, prophets; and some, evangelists; and some, pastors and teachers;

12. For the perfecting of the saints, for the work of the ministry, for the edifying of the body of Christ:

13. Till we all come in the unity of the faith, and of the knowledge of the Son of God, unto a perfect man, unto the measure of the stature of the fullness of Christ:

14. That we henceforth be no more children, tossed to and fro, and carried about with

every wind of doctrine, by the sleight of men, and cunning craftiness, whereby they lie in wait to deceive;

15. But speaking the truth in love, may grow up into him in all things, which is the head, even Christ:

15. But speaking the truth in love, may grow up into him in all things, which is the head, even Christ:

THE GIFT OF PROPHECY An Introduction to the Prophetic Gift

Notes:

THE GIFT OF PROPHECY
An Introduction to the Prophetic Gift

www.ingramcontent.com/pod-product-compliance
Lightning Source LLC
Chambersburg PA
CBHW050344010526
44119CB00049B/688